W9-BMI-146

THE CHANGING STATUS OF GERMAN REUNIFICATION IN WESTERN DIPLOMACY 1955–1966

Studies in International Affairs Number 4

Studies in International Affairs Number 4

THE CHANGING STATUS OF GERMAN REUNIFICATION IN WESTERN DIPLOMACY 1955-1966

by Charles R. Planck

Washington Center of Foreign Policy Research
School of Advanced International Studies
The Johns Hopkins University

The Johns Hopkins Press, Baltimore, Maryland

FOREWORD

In Europe every important issue of international politics is entangled with the historic "German problem." That problem has many facets. Broadly it is: how to contain Germany's energies in a manner that will reassure its wary neighbors, yet guarantee national expression and security; how to keep Germany's political weight in balance with the rest of Europe, yet avoid the dangerous frustrations that might accompany its diplomatic isolation. The postwar division of Germany did not create this problem, but it has greatly accentuated it.

When West Germany joined NATO in 1954, the allies undertook a formal commitment to pursue German reunification in negotiations with the Communist bloc. The formula then envisaged involved a climatic negotiation between East and West. By 1967 the conditions affecting Germany's position in Europe have changed greatly. The commitment to reunification remains, but Germany and its allies have now adopted a new formula in which reunification is seen as occurring as the result of a long-run process of bridge-building between East and West.

Mr. Planck's essay analyzes the essential background of the current developments in the status of German reunification. He examines the major junctures in East-West diplomacy after Germany joined NATO—the Geneva Summit Conference, the Soviet compaign for détente, the Berlin crisis, Kennedy's and de Gaulle's initiatives in Europe—from the perspective of Bonn's efforts to maintain the commitment to reunification. Western unity was most complete at the Geneva meeting of 1955. Thereafter interallied disagreement on the role of German unity in a final European settlement increased, while Bonn, because of its extreme dependence on allied support, continued to stress a uniformity of interests in reunification. Periods of difficult readjustment were frequent, and the measure of success became not whether Western interests in German unity were identical but whether they could be viewed as compatible. Increasingly, the Federal Republic has had to devise a more independent and flexible policy, suited to a looser community of interests. The West German experience mirrors the transitional state of all Western thought concerning such questions as disarmament, European security arrangements, and the future of East-West relations. This essay is part of the Center's continuing effort to interpret the mingling of old and new elements in basic international trends.

Charles R. Planck is a candidate for the degree of doctor of philosophy in international relations at The Johns Hopkins University School of Advanced International Studies and research assistant in the School's Washington Center of Foreign Policy Research.

March, 1967   ROBERT E. OSGOOD
                     Director
                     Washington Center of Foreign
                     Policy Research

CONTENTS

THE CHANGING STATUS OF GERMAN REUNIFICATION IN WESTERN DIPLOMACY 1955–1966

Studies in International Affairs Number 4

I. INTRODUCTION

Since 1954 the Federal Republic of Germany has explicitly declared itself dependent on allied support for the achievement of both security and national reunification. In treaties and in actions, Bonn has consistently sought the defense of West Germany only within the framework of NATO, reunification only within the framework of broader Western policies toward the Communist bloc. All the countries of postwar Europe have, in varying degrees, questioned and compromised the ideal of national sovereignty. But the Federal Republic's decision to rely on external powers and institutions transcending national borders has been unique, both in its extent and in its formality.

A recent paper by Uwe Nerlich traces the implications for German foreign policy of this dependence in the realm of security.[1] Within the limits of certain formal restrictions mainly related to atomic weapons, and subject to more general allied suspicion of its intentions, the Bonn government has encountered a series of difficulties in pursuing a policy of full integration in a military alliance increasingly reliant on nuclear weapons in a period of rapidly shifting strategic doctrine. But, since Bonn considered full participation in NATO defense vital to its security, it was unwilling to forego the policy of integration, even when this conflicted with the goal of

[1] Uwe Nerlich, "Die nuklearen Dilemmas der Bundesrepublik Deutschland," *Europa Archiv*, 10 September 1965, p. 637–52.

reassuring its new partners of Germany's peaceful intentions. Moreover, because the Paris agreements formally granted Germany a role as a fully equal partner in Western defense in return for a crucial West German military contribution, Bonn considered the policy of integration a just, as well as a necessary, fulfillment of a bargain.

Comparable problems have beset German policy concerning reunification. Here, too, there are contractual commitments between the Federal Republic and its allies that reflect overlapping interests. West Germany's task has been to maintain the solemn allied commitment to seek its national unity at times when the allies were following other, perhaps contradictory, goals in East-West relations. Allied support was considered indispensable, but it might be lost if German efforts to equate reunification with the political purpose of the NATO alliance were too insistent, restrictive, or demanding. As in the area of defense policy, however, Bonn saw no hope in a unilateral course, and the chronic strains accompanying the pursuit of unity within an allied framework had to be faced. Although the bargain of the 1954 agreements was the basis for all West German policy, caution had to be exercised so that efforts to hold the allies to that bargain did not become counterproductive.

The achievement of German unity was for the Federal Republic a prime national goal. For the other allies it was at best only an indirect facet of the national interest. Drawing upon all possible means to maintain the necessary diplomatic and military backing in pursuit of its goal, Bonn was prone to stress an identity of interests in reunification that disregarded the disparities inherent in separate national concerns. Periods of difficult re-adjustment to new allied policies were accordingly frequent, during which the measure of success gradually came to be not whether Western interests were identical, but whether they could be viewed as compatible. So great were Germany's military vulnerability and diplomatic insecurity, however, that a determined adherence to policies and arrangements deriving from days of relatively high cohesion in the alliance was more characteristic of Bonn's policy than that of other allies, who came to question the pertinence of NATO to their basic concerns.

This paper will review the course of NATO policy on German reunification from the perspective of West German preferences and Bonn's endeavors to have them respected in the diplomatic efforts of the major allies. Central to the debate among the main partners in the alliance has been the question of what place German reunification should have in a final European settlement. Related questions concern the nature of disarmament and new security commitments to accompany a settlement, and the priority to be accorded among the several problem areas, political, military, and institutional, in the search for East-West agreements. The issues, then, are a definition of the ideal elements of a more stable European order, and the proper sequence for implementing a détente.

NATO AND THE GERMAN REUNIFICATION PROBLEM

The Allied Settlement with Germany of 1954

The decision to include West Germany in NATO in 1954 was the consummation of the conception of an alliance backed by American power to defend Western Europe against the Soviet Union. As the cold war intensified in concrete disagreements over the treatment of Germany, it was only a matter of time until the evolving society that the allies nurtured in their zones of occupation would be accepted as an ally instead of a protectorate. Moreover, at the same time that Germany was admitted as a fully equal partner in Western defenses, the allies made a binding commitment to support reunification as a "fundamental goal" of their diplomacy. The formal extension of the alliance to its natural defensive perimeter occurred simultaneously with the formal assumption of a pledge to extend Western political influence beyond that perimeter. The completion of an alliance championed from its inception as defensive involved the reassertion of revisionist political goals.

It was one thing for the Western allies—America, Britain and France—to subscribe in a vague and tentative manner, at various times during and after the war, to the ideal of a Germany reunited along democratic lines. It was quite another to make a similar commitment in clear and contractual form to a German government actually functioning in one part of the country and openly challenging the legitimacy of a well-ensconced administration on German soil across the border. The Paris agreements constituted in their entirety the Western peace settlement with West Germany. It was a separate peace, in which a recovered and reformed German government converted its former enemies in the West into allies and obtained their support in continuing the struggle with its Eastern foe for control of the rest of the country. The allied undertaking was all the more weighty since the West German government was providing in return an army that its partners, especially the United States, considered indispensable for its own and Europe's security.

Not only the broad give and take of the settlement but its several particulars must be kept in view to convey completely the nature and extent of the commitment by NATO to the goal of German reunification. First and most fundamental, the former occupying powers undertook in the Paris agreements to accord the Federal Republic "the full authority of a sovereign State over its internal and external affairs," and to apply the "principle of sovereign equality" as defined by the United Nations Charter in all their relationships with West Germany. This acknowledgment was no mere formality in the eyes of the West German government. It gave the nation back its political life, whatever the accompanying limitations and qualifications might be. Second, the allies accepted the West German government as sovereign not only within its own juridical borders, but as the sole legitimate spokesman for the whole German people. This implied a joint policy of nonrecognition of the East German regime, which could not be abandoned without violating the sovereignty of the Federal Republic, since its very raison d'être as expressed in the federal constitution was to repre-

sent all Germany until a truly national government
was formed. Third, the allies declared that the
"achievement through peaceful means of a fully
free and unified Germany remains a fundamental
goal of their policy," and stipulated expressly that
no decision on the borders of a future Germany
could be made except by means of a peace treaty
freely negotiated with an all-German government.
This entailed a refusal to grant the finality of the
Oder-Neisse border, less because it was the result
of a fait accompli by the Soviet Union that contributed to the failure of postwar cooperation than
because such a recognition would constitute for the
West's new ally a fateful reversion to the practice
of a dictated peace. Fourth, the determination to
defend allied presence in Berlin was reiterated.[2]
Here, too, a policy previously adhered to in the
over-all evolution of the containment doctrine was
integrated into a series of pledges to the West German government, which followed the more specific
goal of marshaling and making permanent allied
support for the national task of achieving reunification.

In return for this complex of allied undertakings
on its behalf, the Federal Republic accepted a
burden and submitted to certain limitations. The
burden entailed the provision of 500,000 troops for
NATO defenses. The limitations on its sovereignty
in general and on its specific role in military affairs
were several. Unilaterally, West Germany made a
three-point declaration of peaceful intentions, to the
effect that it would (1) conduct its policies in ac-

[2] *NATO, Facts about the North Atlantic Treaty Organization* (Paris: NATO Information Service, January, 1962), pp.
233–59.

cordance with the provisions of the U.N. Charter, (2) refrain from any actions inconsistent with the defensive character of the Western defense treaties, and (3) never resort to force in the pursuit of unity or the modification of existing borders. In the military field, the Federal Republic renounced the manufacture of atomic, biological, or chemical weapons in its own territory, and, within the framework of the Western European Union arms control agency, agreed to major restrictions on the production of other "offensive" arms. All its military forces were to be integrated in NATO defense planning.

For their part, the allies expressed certain reservations on the extent of German sovereignty. The former occupying powers retained their rights and responsibilities inherited from the war relating to Berlin and Germany as a whole, including reunification and a peace settlement. They preserved residual troop stationing privileges, consistent with the maximum possible participation of Germany as an equal partner in the alliance. All of the NATO allies associated themselves with a proviso that were Germany to resort to force in violation of the principles of the Charter or of the defensive character of the alliance, it would forego the right of assistance under the treaty and face joint action by the other members to prevent its becoming a threat to their peace and security. This warning capped the several efforts to reconcile the incorporation of an ally openly dissatisfied with the political status quo into a military organization excessively self-conscious about its defensive origins and purposes.

With the accession to NATO the West German government under Adenauer continued its policy of rehabilitating the German people in the eyes of the

Western political community by playing a willing and sometimes leading role in joint ventures whose purpose was said to transcend the nation-state. The limitations on armament and promises of peaceful behavior involved in the 1954 bargain were considered necessary gestures of good faith to the Federal Republic's new allies. Within their bounds, Germany was entitled both to a fully sovereign and equal role in the evolution of military arrangements providing for the collective defense and to the collective backing of her allies in the pursuit of reunification. German territory was securely covered by the NATO shield, German armed forces were welcomed as an integral part of its strength, and Germany's primary national objective was fully incorporated into the diplomacy of the NATO partners.

During the years 1950–55, when the question of Germany's rearmament and international status was still undecided, the Federal Republic had been at one with the United States in resisting the idea of high level talks with the Russians, favored predominantly by the British. Once the Western defense system was consolidated, however, pressure for negotiations became irresistible. The three Western allies, in close cooperation with West Germany, issued an invitation to the Soviets for a summit conference just five days after the Federal Republic formally entered NATO.

Reunification and East-West Relations in 1955

The base year for any consideration of the role of the reunification problem in recent East-West diplomacy is 1955. At the heads of state and foreign ministers conferences of the summer and fall, each side elaborated with great persistence its basic stance on the preconditions for a safe and stable European political order. The positions established in 1955 provided the dominant theme for all discussions of a European settlement in the subsequent decade.

The Geneva summit approached during a period when the Russians' apparently more conciliatory posture on a range of international issues had fostered high but unspecific hopes for a significant East-West détente. Of particular note had been the agreement on an Austrian peace treaty. It prompted a favorable mention by President Eisenhower in the weeks before the conference of the concept of a neutral belt of armed states in Central Europe as a possible solution to the cold war. This reference to the "Austrian model" aroused a flurry of diplomatic activity in the West that resulted in a clear public delineation of the principles and priorities that would determine the Western position. Immediately, the President's remark was qualified by Secretary of State Dulles, who said that the idea of armed neutrality had no relevance whatever to the future of Germany. Chancellor Adenauer seconded Dulles's view, emphasizing that his country's assumption of NATO membership was in no sense an act to be bargained away for reunification, but rather a prerequisite to achieving it. He won allied endorsement of the German view that reunification by free elections and disarmament in Europe must be negotiated simultaneously, and that additional European security arrangements could only be devised after the re-establishment of German unity. Adenauer did not assert the need for a direct link between reunification and American efforts to reach a general and complete disarmament accord with Russia, the pros-

GERMAN REUNIFICATION

pects for which were held to have improved considerably in view of the surprisingly moderate tenor of recent Soviet proposals. He granted that such an agreement would contribute to an eventual solution of his country's division.

The commitment to reunification in the Paris treaties involved only two specific guides to actual policy: the refusal to recognize the legitimacy of the East German regime and the refusal to recognize the finality of Germany's current borders. Adenauer's accomplishment prior to the conference was to make this essentially defensive stance on German unity operational by stipulating more fully the procedure and substance of a possible settlement. He made reunification the centerpiece of Western diplomacy in a time of détente.

President Eisenhower set forth the dominant and enduring propositions in the first Western speech at the summit:

> Germany is still divided. That division does a grievous wrong to a people which is entitled, like any other, to pursue together a common destiny. While that division continues, it creates a basic source of instability in Europe. Our talk of peace has little meaning if at the same time we perpetuate conditions endangering the peace. . . . In the interest of enduring peace, our solution should take account of the legitimate security interests of all concerned. That is why we insist a united Germany is entitled at its choice, to exercise its inherent right of collective self-defense. By the same token, we are ready to take account of the legitimate security interests of the Soviet Union.[3]

[3] Great Britain, Foreign Office, *Documents Relating to the Meeting of Heads of Government of France, the United Kingdom, the Soviet Union, and the United States of America,* Geneva, July 18–23, 1955, Cmd. 9543 (London: Her Majesty's Stationery Office, July, 1955), p. 7–8.

Eisenhower was prone to emphasize that the existing functions of NATO as a source of peace and the Western European Union (WEU) as a constraint on West Germany's military freedom would basically ensure that even a reunited Germany within these organizations would not be an added threat to European peace or Russian security. His colleague, Eden, concentrated on the additional assurances that the West would offer the Russians if they accepted a plan for German unity through free elections. These might include force limitations and even a certain amount of demilitarization in Central Europe, as well as new security commitments between East and West embodying an implicit pledge to meet in common any renewal of German aggression. These commitments, however, would only be superimposed on the prevailing alliance structure, although it would be somewhat modified by the arms agreements foreseen. Eden's conception of a German settlement was a reapplication of the Locarno idea, which aimed at "combining security for allies with restraints on them and stability for the system as a whole."[4]

More generally, the Western position that security measures had to be accompanied by the simultaneous solution of political disputes rested on the view that the armed confrontation in Europe resulted primarily from a prior conflict of political wills. Subordinated, if not ignored, was the premise behind proposals for simple disarmament that some portion of the accumulated military force was less attributable to the persistent dispute over Germany

[4] George Liska, *Nations in Alliance* (Baltimore: The Johns Hopkins Press, 1962), p. 36.

than to the inner dynamic of an arms race with modern weapons. In the Western view, any reduction of arms would require a stable political base to be safe and lasting; the acknowledged sources of conflict would have to be eliminated, or the fear of attack and hence the justification for arms would remain. The ideal proposal was a package one, which carefully linked progress toward political compromise with reductions in the actual means of waging war.

Leeway for maneuver outside the preferred Western package was practically nonexistent. Eden's proposal at another juncture of the conference for a simple inspection zone on either side of the prevailing demarcation line was politically distasteful to America in particular, because it seemed to imply that the situation on the continent was sufficiently stable to be accepted de facto as the starting point for lasting relaxation. And the cool allied response, both to French Premier Faure's speculation on a partial dissolution of blocs occurring after German reunification and to the concept of armed neutrality alluded to earlier by Eisenhower, demonstrated that the content of the package itself was even less subject to modification.

Russian policy on the content and sequence of a Central European settlement stood in radical opposition. Premier Bulganin arrived in Geneva with various proposals to retard, if not reverse, the process of West German rearmament and incorporation into the NATO system. Initially, Bulganin concentrated his efforts in support of a European security pact to replace NATO and the Warsaw Treaty Organization (WTO). Institution of the pact would have been accompanied by a halt of the Federal

Republic's rearmament, the initiation of foreign troop and base withdrawals in all of Europe, and extensive worldwide disarmament measures. The new arrangement was to include two separate German states until the creation of a single Germany. Bulganin's guiding premise was that the

> . . . easing of tension in international relations and the creation of an effective system of security in Europe would largely facilitate the settlement of the German problem and would bring about the necessary prerequisites for the unification of Germany on peaceful and democratic principles. . . . It must be admitted that the remilitarization of Western Germany and its integration into military groupings of the Western Powers now represents the main obstacle to its unification.[5]

This package was unacceptable as a whole, both because it violated the several allied propositions about Germany's right to national unity and a free foreign and defense policy and because it challenged the entire framework of Western security arrangements in Europe. But even when the Russian proposals were presented separately, without reference to the evolution of a new European security pact, they were rejected. All the individual suggestions that the Soviets put forward at the two Geneva conferences —troop cuts in Germany, more general zones of arms limitation and inspection in Central Europe, a nonaggression commitment between WTO and NATO, the formation of all-German committees— suffered in Western eyes from the same basic liability. They either sought to begin dismantling Western defenses before the real source of instability, the

[5] *Documents Relating to the Meeting of Heads of Government*, p. 22–23.

German division, was removed, or they tended to perpetuate the division itself. Every Western pronouncement on European affairs at the 1955 meetings reiterated the necessity for a firm link between disarmament and German reunification. The NATO allies were in Geneva to argue for the one settlement upon which a lasting, cumulative détente could be based.

Thus it was considered a victory for Western diplomacy, despite the total lack of substantive agreement, that the Soviet Premier affixed his signature to the Geneva Directives, which restated the "common responsibility" of the Big Four for the settlement of the German question by means of free elections, and acknowledged the "close link between the reunification of Germany and the problem of European security and the fact that the successful settlement of each of these problems would serve the interests of consolidating peace."[6] Whatever interpretations the Soviets subsequently chose to read into the Directives, the West felt with good reason that they constituted a valuable statement of its basic position on the preconditions for a stable European order, a welcome supplement to the lamentably vague and increasingly distant Potsdam accords. They formed the East-West counterpart to the Paris agreements.

Still it is not customary to view the Geneva sessions on Germany as a positive achievement at all, but rather as the last of the long series of postwar conferences on the country's future. It is argued that after the futile confrontation of manifestly incompatible designs for the continent, the Soviet Union

[6] *Ibid.*, pp. 29–30.

took the final steps to establish East Germany as a separate regime, and the West proceeded with the policy of rearming and integrating the Federal Republic in NATO defenses, a course whose ultimate effect was to cement the division just as finally as the Eastern actions. This interpretation has the virtues of realism and simplicity. But even if eventually correct in its essentials, it fails to indicate the extent to which the priority accorded by the West in 1955 to the achievement of reunification had an operative influence on major junctures in East-West diplomacy as well as on the development of the NATO alliance in the succeeding decade. The premises of 1955 provided a main functioning guideline for Western policy until 1960, they complicated infinitely the efforts of Presidents Kennedy and de Gaulle to explore new paths in East-West relations after 1960, and they remain crucially relevant today to any consideration of how the European stalemate may evolve.

Thus the arguments of the Western statesmen must be seen as more than simply pro forma justifications to the Soviets and to world opinion of Germany's integrationist course. Eisenhower and his colleagues genuinely believed that the solution to the German problem evolved by the West since 1949 was the only sensible means of treating a potentially great and disruptive power. The logic behind the Coal and Steel Community and European army proposals is familiar enough. However implausible it was to assume that the Soviets would accept the Geneva suggestions, it is even more implausible to expect that the West would have abandoned the integration formula and its rationale in a major confrontation of views on the prerequisites of a healthy

European order. Far from being a naïve or hypo-
critical approach to the problems dividing the two
blocs, the Western offers were based on policy principles that had developed over an entire decade and
were not to be abandoned overnight.

The Adenauer government regarded the common
Western stand on Germany as the crowning vindication of the Federal Republic's undeviating westward
course since its foundation. Fidelity to the West had
now resulted in the strongest possible defensive and
diplomatic front to the East. Opposition calls for a
more independent diplomacy were rejected on the
grounds that Bonn was fully represented in all allied
deliberations. More fundamentally, the government's resolute denial of the necessity for a unilateral search for reunification rested on the argument
that only if Germany continued its voluntary cooperation with the West could it fulfill its appointed
task of assuring the existence of a free order on the
continent against the threat of the repugnant political system in the East. If, for example, permanent
neutralization were accepted as the price of reunification, as the Soviets had sometimes suggested, the
country would be at the mercy of East and West
alike in their continuing efforts to strengthen or
weaken it in accord with their prospects of gaining
control. Under such circumstances, a Germany
pressed for its very existence could revert to a dis-
honest policy of playing one side against the other,
a *Schaukelpolitik;* nor would a free domestic order
be possible in the context of such external threats.
This dire logic, which could end either with a Communist takeover or with the re-emergence of Germany as an independent and estranged great power,
was employed by Bonn to demonstrate to allied and

domestic opinion that a reunited Germany could evolve as a stable and reliable political entity only if it were free to continue a natural association with the Western community. An intermediate buffer state status, in which its freedom in foreign and domestic policy were compromised, would produce dangerous insecurity and resentment.

Such reasoning was employed by the Federal Republic after 1955 to convince Western opinion that the model of a Germany reunited with the West rested on enduring mutual interests. It was largely accepted. Politically relevant criticism of Western policy at Geneva and in succeeding years related less to the substance of the settlement proposed than to the interim policies advocated by the Bonn government for attaining it. Since by 1955 the Soviets had ended virtually all references to reunification and had adopted the two-state theory, West Germany's job was not only to defend the ideal settlement envisioned by the West, but to convince its allies and, needless to say, the Soviet Union that nothing short of that settlement, even the tacit acceptance of the status quo, could ever guarantee tranquility in Europe. This involved the question of tactics, of what could be done in the period before a settlement was attained. Given the cardinal assertion that the denial of self-determination to the German people was an injustice on which no stable order could ever be based, continued refusal to grant diplomatic recognition or political respectability to East Germany was the indispensable minimum requirement for holding open the possibility of reunification. Moreover, precisely because the enforced division created the basic instability, while it persisted, disarmament and security measures were also unacceptable lest they shift the military balance against the West before the conflict was resolved, or contribute to a freezing of the intolerable status quo. West Germany must continue to participate in building the free world defenses through NATO, while simultaneously holding out the promise of security concessions to the Soviet Union in return for unity. In that way it would fulfill its legitimate security needs within the WEU restrictions, and prove at the same time that the best guarantee that a reunited Germany would never again misuse its power would be its incorporation into a similar system of restraint in which it would continue to voluntarily forego the possibility of independent action.

The point of great debate was whether wholehearted dedication to the Westward course would leave sufficient room for maneuver and experimentation in the search for a settlement in the East. Bonn considered its unchanging task in the years after Geneva to prove to skeptics in East and West alike that the allied German settlement of 1954 was a workable framework that would some day have to be extended for the necessary all-European regulation of the political and military problems dividing the continent. After the arduous years of regaining sovereignty and respectability for one portion of Germany, the Federal Republic's leaders felt that the longer road to national unity in freedom was just opening up.

The Maintenance of the Reunification Commitment, 1955–60

The operative effects of pursuing the policy on Germany adopted in 1954 and 1955 can be described under three headings: first, the Western response, and attempts at counterinitiatives, to Communist-bloc proposals on disarmament and a political settlement in the period 1956–58; second, Western reactions to the first Soviet ultimatum on Berlin in November, 1958; and third, post-Camp David diplomacy regarding a summit conference.

Disarmament and Détente, 1956–58. Whereas Soviet inflexibility on German reunification was understood by Dulles and Adenauer as a vindication of the Western position, the British and French lamented the extent of the deadlock and arrived at the first disarmament talks after Geneva, which convened in London in March, with plans for a new start. They sought a beginning agreement on great power conventional force reductions so that the imminent rearmament of Germany would not be necessary; its postponement might lead to new measures in the field of European security, thus facilitating reunification. In effect this endorsed the Soviet sequence of priorities, by placing the German issue last. Bonn quickly set about to recreate the clarity and unity of the allied position, declaring itself in favor of controlled general disarmament, while reiterating that that search would ultimately be futile and dangerous if it ignored the German division. Before disarmament began, it was argued, West Germany must attain the minimum military establishment necessary for its security, to which level other nations' forces could be initially reduced; above all, there must be no agreements leading West Germany toward a neutral status.

This elaboration of the Geneva premises into a set of clear priorities resulted in a unified Western statement to the Soviets at the London negotiations

that, in principle, while progress toward general disarmament could certainly begin on the basis of existing political circumstances, completion of the process
would have to await resolution of outstanding political problems. Insistence on this principle added
to the already long list of differences that divided
the two camps in their search for universal disarmament, but its most important effects were felt in the
discussion of European affairs.

For the Soviets, the years after Geneva were a
time of maneuver. They continued to advocate in
the name of peaceful coexistence a series of partial
measures that, while less ambitious than the idea of
a new European security pact, had the same dual
purpose of gaining recognition of the status quo and
preventing NATO's adoption of a nuclear posture,
especially in Germany. The heart of their program
was the suggestion for a nuclear free zone in Central
Europe, first proposed by Gromyko in March, 1956,
and later to become permanently associated with
Polish Foreign Minister Rapacki, who broached a
more concrete plan in October, 1957. This was never
accepted by the West, even as a basis for discussion,
because of the objection in principle to isolated disarmament agreements based on the continuation of
the German division; less fundamental but equally
effective was the objection to discrimination in armament against one ally before the common threat was
overcome. Strategic arguments always complemented
these objections to nuclear free zones, but the primary criterion was political.

The Soviets' major political proposals were two:
the idea of a NATO-WTO nonaggression agreement, rejected by the West because it threatened to
involve the West in diplomatic relations with East

Germany and to imply tacit acceptance of the political and territorial status quo; and the idea of a German Confederation, first put forth by Ulbricht in late 1956, rejected because it formalized the existence of two German states, proposed the execution of radical disarmament measures as a prerequisite for progress toward unity, and contained rules for political relations totally at odds with Western constitutional and democratic practices.

Western objections to the Soviet program for détente were procedural as well as substantive. Calls for a summit conference beginning in the winter of 1958 were resisted in part because the proposed agenda omitted all reference to reunification as a matter of four-power responsibility according to the Geneva directives.

Defensiveness to this degree inspired criticism within the Western camp as well. The course of disengagement advocated with mounting insistence after 1955 by opposition spokesmen in Germany, Britain, and America questioned both the sequence of the officially favored settlement, by putting denuclearization and foreign troop withdrawals at the head of the process, and its substance, by proposing a semi-detached status for a reunited Germany between the blocs. With varying emphasis, these critics upheld the demand for German unity through free elections, but the loose-linked process allegedly leading to that goal was considered too risky in the interim, too vague in the long run, by the Western statesmen in power.

One measure in the realm of arms control and disarmament thought to be applicable to Europe prior to a reunification agreement was the conception of an inspection zone to guard against surprise attack. Under American initiative, the West advanced in 1957 several proposals for air and ground observation. These did not invalidate the principle that actual arms reductions in Europe demanded concurrent political progress; they were not limited to European territory alone, but very pointedly included strategically significant areas of Russian soil; and they did not center on the prevailing demarcation line. Nevertheless, even the process of exploring, with such elaborate precautions, simple force inspection on the continent put immense strains on the American-German relationship.

The inclination of the chief American negotiator, Stassen, to engage in tête-à-têtes with the Soviet delegates occasioned the first serious suspicion in Germany of a great-power deal on Europe. German diplomacy in this period worked actively to prevent that possibility, and a series of allied declarations such as the following communiqué from an Adenauer-Eisenhower meeting revealed the severe limits that past policy had set to a more flexible search for arms agreements in Europe:

> The President stressed that any measures for disarmament applicable to Europe would be accepted by the United States only with the approval of the NATO allies, which he hoped would take a leading role in this regard, and taking into account the link between European security and German reunification. He assured the Chancellor that the United States does not intend to take any action in the field of disarmament which would prejudice the reunification of Germany.
>
> The President and the Chancellor agreed that, if a beginning could be made toward more effective measures of disarmament, this would create a degree of confidence which would facilitate further progress in the field of dis-

armament and in the settlement of outstanding major
political problems such as the reunification of Germany.[7]

Allied efforts to seize the initiative in the political field did not gain great attention, much less a
positive Russian response. In a series of major notes
to the Soviet Union, Bonn underlined in vain its
willingness to make concessions on disarmament and
European security in return for reunification, pre-
ferring this type of coherent reiteration of NATO's
policy on Germany to the tactic of gingerly holding
political issues in abeyance while investigating prom-
ising first steps in other areas. Even a modest procedural proposal, the joint Western call for a stand-
ing four-power commission to work out common
suggestions for a solution to the German question,
was evaded by the Soviets.

In the two years after 1955 the Russians suc-
ceeded neither in gaining recognition of the political
status quo nor in inaugurating any diminution of
NATO's military strength through separate agreements. They had forced the West to concentrate increasingly on the tactics of holding open the possibility of its desired settlement in lieu of substantive
negotiations, but this was only a negative gain. Thus
Soviet diplomacy reverted in November, 1958, from
the language of détente to ultimatum in a bold effort
to force concessions on the political issues lying at
the core of the European conflict.

*Berlin and the Geneva Foreign Ministers Con-
ference.* The belligerent Soviet declarations of late

[7] U.S., Department of State Publication 7008, *Documents on
Disarmament,* 1945–59 (2 vols.; Washington: U.S. Government
Printing Office, August, 1960), II, p. 790.

1958, threatening to convert West Berlin into a neutral and demilitarized city and to transfer the control of Western access rights to a sovereign East German regime unless the four occupying powers could agree jointly on such arrangements within six months, had the initial effect of reopening East-West talks on German unity. While rejecting vigorously the idea of negotiations under pressure and Russia's intention of abrogating unilaterally any aspect of four-power responsibility, the allies did offer to engage in talks at the foreign ministers level, provided that they treat the "problem of Germany in all its aspects and implications," which meant precisely reunification, European security, and a peace treaty in that order. Berlin was simply added to European security and disarmament as another issue that could only be satisfactorily solved in the context of German unity. This time, however, the NATO powers were unable to display the unity and consistency on Germany that had characterized their position four years earlier.

Even before the conference convened there were signs that the premises and priorities of past years were being called into question. Dulles's remarks that East German officials might be acceptable as "agents" of the Soviet Union in controlling access, and that free elections were not necessarily the only conceivable way to unity, threatened the heart of Bonn's policy: nonrecognition of the Soviet zone and the inalienable right of self-determination. On a hurried trip to Moscow and Western capitals in early 1959, Macmillan propagated limited disarmament schemes in Central Europe to be coupled with a confederation leading gradually to reunification. This, too, indicated how skeptical Western statesmen had become about the realism of reproposing the optimal settlement of 1955.

Especially significant was Macmillan's desire to convey to the Soviet Union the Western determination to defend its rights in Berlin, while probing at the same time for ways to make that presence more palatable. Two years later, the American government under Kennedy made a similar search. Under Kennedy, the demand for firm guarantees for West Berlin came gradually to replace the former insistence on German reunification as a prerequisite for consideration of other security arrangements in Central Europe. At the time of Macmillan's efforts, the search for a new Berlin agreement was conducted as a more isolated undertaking. To negotiate primarily on Berlin was to accept the Soviet definition of the sources of tension in Europe; to concentrate in these talks on defending the substance of Western rights in the city without due regard to the implications of the form of a possible new agreement on the legal and political status of the existing order was to compromise further the Western position. After 1959, Bonn repeatedly felt the need to call attention to these risks.

The Herter plan for reunification, the West's opening bid, was a tightly-knit package of interrelated political and military measures. It departed not in form but in content from the previous allied position, by postponing free elections for a two and one-half year transition period and instituting a good measure of disarmament and additional East-West security pledges before reunion occurred. West German officials endorsed the plan for its logic and the inseparability of its provisions, but were careful to point out that, especially in its confederal tendencies, it represented a maximum in concessions to Soviet desires.

Nonetheless, the feeling was practically universal in 1959 that the presentation by each side of its respective German plan was a mere formality. The Soviets had defined the key issue. The West, in consenting to discuss Berlin's status separately, granted implicitly that instability derived from circumstances other than the lack of a general German settlement. One interim proposal foreseeing the city's union in the context of the Herter plan was rejected by the Soviets out of hand. A second, acknowledging the absence of agreement on reunification, reconfirmed allied access rights but contained major concessions by allowing East German personnel to administer access, by limiting allied garrisons in the city, and by establishing rules against hostile propaganda issuing from either sector. Despite these efforts to placate Russian demands, it fared no better. The Soviet charge of Berlin's "abnormality" was indirectly conceded.

Deadlocked at every point, the ministers meeting in Geneva chose as occasion for adjournment the announcement of Khrushchev's coming visit to America. In a final effort to revive the 1958 idea of a four-power commission to discuss reunification, the West proposed that the foreign ministers forum be kept in existence, but the Soviets predictably objected. Thus ended the last formal conference of the postwar period dedicated to the "problem of Germany in all its aspects and implications," although the narrower issue of Berlin was far from dead. Thereafter, Western diplomacy was less certain than ever in defining a common focal point for negotiations with the Communist camp.

Camp David to the 1960 Summit. The only concrete outcome of the Camp David meeting was
Eisenhower's assent in principle to a Big Four summit, after which there ensued a most complicated
period of intra-Western deliberations over whether
to talk and what to talk about. The British were
extremely desirous both of high-level negotiations
and of proceeding with the Berlin suggestions made
at the close of the foreign ministers conference. The
United States was not so positively inclined to a
summit as the British, but found it unavoidable, and
tended to support a more reluctant Germany in the
argument that the basis for talks should be the
Herter plan. France under de Gaulle was unenthusi-
astic for various reasons and also tended to back
the German position on how to proceed. The Adenauer government became progressively apprehen-
sive that reunification as a distinct topic would be
dropped from the agenda and, in a tactical maneuver to avoid discussions limited only to Berlin, tried
to direct attention away from European issues entirely toward general disarmament as a topic for
the summit. Defense of the position elaborated in
1955 continued to ensure Western rejection of Communist proposals on disarmament in Europe, and
the "three Germanies" concept implicit in the Berlin demands. But consensus on the contents of an
alternative Germany plan was fading, and differences were obvious on how best to counter Soviet
tactics as they switched from ultimata to summitry
and back again. Indicative of the endemic allied
disagreement is the fact that prior to the abortive
summit of May, 1960, no clear announcement was
ever made on whether an interim Berlin agreement
was to be sought anew.

70396

As the Eisenhower years drew to a close, there were indications that the maintenance of the reunification commitment was becoming a matter of rhetoric to a greater degree than it had been in the past. At the 1959 Geneva sessions, Western delegates reportedly intimated in private to the Communist spokesmen that abandonment of the nonrecognition policy was impossible for the time being, because of the realities of West German domestic opinion. In a public comment of the same time, de Gaulle coupled a strong endorsement of German unity with explicit reference to existing borders. More generally, the now familiar conviction had grown in some Western circles that undue deference to the Adenauer government's preferences granted Germany a veto on all efforts to reduce East-West tension. These Western observers saw only a dangerous mixture for perpetuating the division of Europe and its accompanying tensions in the lack of clear statements from West Germany to the Czech and Polish governments on border claims, in Bonn's resistance to separate Berlin and disarmament agreements, and in continued German pursuit of integration into NATO's nuclear defenses.

The Federal Republic's allies, America under Dulles foremost among them, did not make such judgments public. But it does seem that they had come, in the years between 1955 and 1960, to defend Bonn's positions less in the conviction that these would someday bring about the ideal settlement proposed than in the interest of preventing German disaffection from the Western camp that was feared if the options theoretically necessary to hold open the possibility of that settlement were foreclosed one by one. This was, surely, one of the original motives for accepting Germany into the alliance and the European communities: to prevent the country from ever again desiring an independent course in external affairs. Bonn's Western orientation was never held to be an end in itself, however, but only a means to a reunification agreement that would create a truly stable, because more just, basis for European order. Now, after fifteen years of fruitless argument with the Soviets over this issue, five of them with the Federal Republic as an ally, the temptation had grown for the Western powers to view the interim solution to the German problem as a satisfactory one, and to render rhetorical support for the ideal solution primarily in order to preserve the prevailing arrangement. After all, the West Germans themselves seemingly asked for little more than ritualistic reaffirmations of increasingly empty slogans.

That there was a certain amount of hypocrisy and self-delusion in this development, has been commonly remarked. And yet, given the unchanging need to keep the Federal Republic a satisfied and friendly power in the interests of long-term balance and stability in Europe, some hypocrisy was unavoidable, since the division could be neither overcome nor legitimized. The 1955 theses on Germany's right to national unity could, for a time, be ignored in practice, but never repudiated in public. Despite their excessive formality, and, in some respects, almost aggressive ring, the theses still stood for the principles of sound statesmanship that the Western allies felt should be applied in determining a great nation's political future. Even more candid and concerted efforts in the 1960's to reach agreements with the Russians in Central Europe proved this point:

Three diplomatic assaults from the West on the German division and its related armament and security problems, led by Dulles, Kennedy, and de Gaulle, each with differing degrees of West German support, still leave the continent with what must be termed a provisional situation.

THE UNITED STATES AND GERMAN
REUNIFICATION—1961–63

---

*Kennedy's Experimentation with Inherited Policies
in the Berlin Crisis, 1961–62*

The Kennedy administration was committed to a
policy of arms control in the broad sense of design-
ing coherent policies to stabilize the essentially bipolar balance of power. This entailed efforts to
achieve a more flexible and controlled defense posture for the Western world and to establish better
communications with the Communist world. The
goal was, at a minimum, to prevent miscalculation
leading to war in the continuing cold war struggle;
at a maximum, to reach agreements beginning in the
military realm to go beyond hostile coexistence to
peaceful cooperation. The program proved itself
insufficiently attuned to the European environment.
America's allies resisted the troop increases that the
new strategy demanded, while the efforts to prevent
the growth of additional centers of nuclear power
dismayed proponents of a NATO nuclear force and
French policy-makers alike. The prospective Russian
partner was less interested in sophisticated theories
of arms control at the strategic level than in the
burning political issues centering on Germany. Rum-
blings over Berlin were heard very early in 1961,
and Kennedy's Vienna meeting with Khrushchev
announced the real beginning of long and laborious
efforts to apply a broad and bipolar strategy for
East-West relations to a complicated European crisis
involving the interests of several powers.

The Kennedy administration's response to the new Russian threat of a separate peace treaty with Ulbricht to end allied rights in Berlin was different from that of its predecessor, both militarily and diplomatically. To avoid miscalculation of Western determination and to augment the applicable military force available in Europe, Kennedy ordered an ostentatious execution of long-planned force build-ups during the 1961 crisis. Although Kennedy declined to declare a national emergency and institute general mobilization, this course contrasted directly with America's reluctance in 1958, when faced with a similar ultimatum, to bolster local or strategic forces.

Negotiations with the Russians were sought not so much because they were an unavoidable means of publicizing Soviet intransigence over Germany—Kennedy considered reunification an "unrealistic" objective—but because a willingness to talk would prevent the crisis from going completely out of control and give America a chance to place issues other than Khrushchev's bellicose demands on the agenda.

On possible responses to the building of the Berlin wall, there was no significant cleavage of allied opinion; some Soviet action to stop the flow of refugees was anticipated, almost welcomed as a step to cool down the crisis. Since it is clear that every aspect of the allied position in Berlin is only more or less militarily untenable, this decision was based less on a judgment of the infeasibility of vigorous counteraction than on the argument that the wall was essentially a defensive action to shore up a vital sphere of Soviet influence. All Western pronouncements (and contingency plans) dealt with possible threats to West Berlin (i.e., another blockade), in an effort to make crystal clear the extent of allied determination. From Germany's standpoint this was a regrettable necessity for, by concentrating on West Berlin, the alliance seemed to grant the Soviet Union a free hand to abrogate unilaterally other aspects of four-power responsibility for the whole city. In the course of making the commitment clear, it was also necessary to make it limited, and this had no doubt eased the Soviet decision to seal off their sector.

After the wall, there continued the delicate and dangerous task of resisting further Soviet encroachments on allied force movements to and within the city, while a heated Western debate on negotiations proceeded, somewhat independently. Intent on overcoming what it considered the traditional rigidity of Western proposals for Europe, the Kennedy government pressed hard for the early development of a negotiating position for a four-power conference and, when faced with persistent disunity, gradually decided to seek exploratory talks with the Soviets, even without allied participation. Eisenhower had welcomed the Camp David session as a low pressure respite from the pace of Big Four diplomacy; Kennedy sought out bilateral talks as a necessary means of speeding it up.

Throughout, the British were wholehearted proponents of one-half of America's strategy; they welcomed every effort to arrive at a new agreement on Berlin, whether coupled with wider disarmament and security measures or not, while resisting calls for a military build-up on the grounds that is might contribute to war panic or ruin the chances for successful talks. At the opposite pole were the French, even more adamantly opposed than in 1959 to negotiations under pressure, for reasons reviewed below. Since none of the allies added significantly to the build-up of American forces backing the diplomatic effort, the French abstention in the diplomatic realm was a greater hindrance to Kennedy's course than was Britain's in the military.

Between these extremes lay West Germany, unable to endorse the British zeal for almost any sort of interim Berlin arrangement, but equally unable to side with the French. Because bilateral discussions on issues vital to it were inevitable, the Federal Republic, to be heard at all, had to make its influence felt through the American position.

Bonn failed from the start to convince the Anglo-American powers to use a modified version of the Herter plan as a basis for four-power talks. For Kennedy, the relevant German question had become the matter of new guarantees for West Berlin, in return for which he was willing to explore ways of making continuation of Western presence and access rights more palatable to the Soviets. Concretely, this meant that such questions as an acceptance of the Oder-Neisse line, a withdrawal of nuclear weapons from the Bundeswehr, the use of East German personnel in checking allied traffic, the possible conversion of Berlin into a U.N.-controlled entity, and even a measure of disengagement in Central Europe were considered. West Germany's reaction at this juncture was to recall the principle that progress toward European security and disarmament had to be linked with progress toward a solution of the whole German problem. Here Bonn had some success, for, after the first round of exploratory bilateral talks in the fall of 1961, America dissociated itself clearly from notions like the Rapacki plan or disengagement.

Still the Adenauer government feared the worst, a far-reaching great-power accord on Central Europe, and stressed on every occasion during that winter that further talks should be limited to Berlin alone, while adducing all available arguments against the necessity of negotiating a new status for the city that would dilute the concept of four-power responsibility and enhance East Germany's position. The situation had deteriorated considerably since 1959, when Bonn thought it might be possible to direct attention away from European matters entirely onto the topic of general disarmament.

Ultimately it became clear that Kennedy was still willing to bargain security measures for Berlin guarantees. The proposed American package of April, 1962, reportedly leaked by Bonn to diminish the prospect of Russian acceptance, contained, in addition to an international access authority giving East Germany and East Berlin equal status with their Western counterparts, the idea of a NATO-WTO nonaggression pact long rejected by the West for political reasons, and a U.S.-U.S.S.R. nonproliferation agreement indicating the priority of great-power concerns over the need for nuclear sharing in NATO. It also called for inter-German committees, but these were not to function under a four-power commission on reunification, as the German government had proposed in the past.

In short, Bonn was faced with the collapse of American support for practically all its major premises on East-West agreements. Only zonal disarmament was ever clearly excluded from the exploratory talks. Other proposals kept reappearing without firm association with reunification. That no agreement emerged from the year of intensive off-and-on bilateral discussions was more a result of the rather surprising Russian unwillingness to consider any text at all conceding a Western presence in Berlin than of de Gaulle's intransigence and of West Germany's ambivalence, bordering frequently on outright opposition to the whole endeavor. Kennedy's guiding conviction of the crucial responsibility of the superpowers to preserve world peace caused him to ride roughshod over allied discontent and to ignore provocative Soviet harassment in Berlin while seeking all possible ways to achieve a stabler modus vivendi in Europe. He was not averse to reconsidering suggestions originating in Soviet proposals of the 1950's or to subordinating the legalities of the Berlin position to what he considered its substance. In the end, he had the opportunity to convince himself fully that the Russians were unready for any "normalization" in Europe that was not wholly on their terms. The experience, rather than killing all of Kennedy's hopes for significant East-West agreements, only led him to prepare more carefully the climate and agenda for the next major period of discussions in 1963.

In view of these departures from past policy, it is important to ask how Kennedy's over-all conception of the German problem differed from other leading Western statesmen. In terms of declared goals, Kennedy fully endorsed the basic West German thesis that genuine European stability depended on the achievement of reunification through self-determination. In private, too, he judged the importance of the Berlin crisis in terms worthy of Adenauer or

Dulles at their most pessimistic. Speaking to President Kekonnen of Finland in October, 1961, he said that Soviet policy in Berlin

> ... is designed to neutralize West Germany as a first step in the neutralization of Western Europe. That is what makes the present situation so dangerous. West Germany is the key as to whether Western Europe will be free. ... It is not that we wish to stand on the letter of the law or that we underestimate the dangers of war. But if we don't meet our commitments in Berlin, it will mean the destruction of NATO and a dangerous situation for the whole world. All Europe is at stake in West Berlin.[8]

Moreover, he was as sensitive as Dulles to the fact that the lever for the implementation of these unlimited Soviet goals was the mood in the Federal Republic:

> We do not want to spread that state of melancholy [occasioned in West Germany by the erection of the Wall] by legitimizing the East German regime and stimulating a nationalist revival in West Germany. ... Germany has been divided for sixteen years and will continue to stay divided. The Soviet Union is running an unnecessary risk in trying to change this from an accepted fact into a legal state. Let the Soviet Union keep Germany divided on its present basis and not try to persuade us to associate ourselves legally with the division and thus weaken our ties to West Germany and their ties to Western Europe.[9]

The difference in Kennedy's position is clear, for half of his remarks would justify a rigid adherence to past positions, admitting of no need to negotiate, with the maintenance of West German confidence

[8] Arthur M. Schlesinger, Jr., *A Thousand Days* (Boston: Houghton Mifflin Co., 1965), pp. 379–80.
[9] *Ibid.*, pp. 398–99.

the prime concern; but in the other half, he felt compelled to admit that the division would obviously continue, barring a radical shift in Soviet policy, and that he hoped to defuse the unsatisfactory situation as much as possible. In this endeavor he was prepared, as we have seen, to dispense with certain legalities and priorities, in partial disregard of that "state of melancholy" in the Federal Republic that he so clearly judged to be the real danger. Détente, in the sense of achieving a minimum understanding with the Soviets not to slide into war, conflicted with the goal of preserving West Germany as the linchpin of the alliance.

In 1961, the search for a superpower agreement unquestionably had priority over concern for allied unity to a degree unprecedented in the 1950's. This was never more strikingly evident than in an interview Kennedy gave to *Izvestia* in November, only three days after consultation with Adenauer over how the Berlin talks should proceed. Despite reference to fulfillment of the 1955 Directives as the "soundest policy," Kennedy argued that in view of the Soviet refusal to permit reunification, a new international agreement regulating access to West Berlin would produce "peace in this area for years." Then, in the context of refuting Soviet propaganda about the danger of West German revanchism, he stated:

> ... as long as German forces are integrated in NATO ... there is security for all. ... Now, if this situation changed, if Germany developed an atomic capability of its own, if it developed missiles or a strong national army that threatened war, then I would understand your concern, and I would share it. ... If it changed, then it would seem to me

appropriate for the United States and the Soviet Union and others to consider the situation at that time.[10]

These remarks indicated that behind the American pressure for a more flexible negotiating stance that seemed to Bonn at best a recipe for the gradual recognition of the status quo was a general tendency to write off publicly any hopes for unity in the foreseeable future, coupled with acknowledgments, however hypothetical, of the overlapping interests of the great powers in controlling West Germany. Together with the specific course of the long talks over Berlin, they constituted a full-scale challenge to the ingrained premises of the Federal Republic's foreign policy. De Gaulle would speak as bluntly a few years later.

Kennedy's Counteroffensive in East-West Relations, 1963

The course and rationale of Kennedy's steps to reopen a dialogue with the Soviet Union after Cuba are well-known; this account shall focus on the European aspects of the mood of détente that reigned in 1963. Basically, American policy avoided raising the controversial political issues that had plagued the Berlin talks and concentrated on a series of inspection and communication measures designed to lessen the danger of war by surprise attack or miscalculation. In contrast to the 1957 talks, no specific

[10] U.S., Department of State Publication 7808, *American Foreign Policy: Current Documents 1961* (Washington: U.S. Government Printing Office, June, 1965), pp. 668–70.

zonal proposals were formulated; the efforts at Geneva were to a certain degree carried out just to educate the Soviets in more sophisticated matters of arms control, to gain their acceptance of the principle of "inspection without disarmament."

Apart from these talks seeking a starting point for agreements in Europe midway between the Russian call for simple disarmament and the Western formula linking military and political steps, Western policy on "Europeanizing" the détente was largely defensive. Steadfastly rejected were Communist calls for the Rapacki plan and troop cuts in Europe, as were proposals linking ground observation posts with denuclearization in Central Europe. Khrushchev's attempt to tie the test ban to a NATO-WTO nonaggression pact failed as well, since Kennedy and his advisers had become aware of the destabilizing effects of proceeding too quickly in the bilateral search for détente over the heads of the allies.

Thus, when America, with the British in tandem, sought to maintain the much-vaunted "momentum" generated at Moscow, there was little prospect for a return to the traditional Western agenda for Europe. Although the Russians clearly were interested in resuming talks on Berlin and disarmament in Europe, the Americans stressed such issues as observation posts, underground testing, nonproliferation, the production of fissionable materials and, as a priority matter, the peaceful uses of space. Kennedy's strategy was to explore areas of agreement, sufficiently remote from allied interests and the complicated political map of Europe, where superpower cooperation could be practiced and extended. The hope was that success in so-called peripheral or universal measures could create an atmosphere more conducive to a return to the center of the military and political confrontation.

In relating this long-range strategy for détente to the problem of divided Germany, administration spokesmen emphasized that the only sensible course was to accept the division as an enforced reality, which only war could undo, and encourage increased contacts with the eastern zone to better the lot and maintain the hopes of those denied their political rights by the Soviet system. West Berlin and West Germany would serve as a daily demonstration that the Western way of life combined the elemental democratic freedoms with economic well-being. Ultimately, if Germany and the rest of Europe made common cause with the United States in evolving an Atlantic Partnership with close ties to the third world, the day would come when the Soviet leaders would realize the impossibility and danger of upholding their pretensions to world domination, and the policy of keeping Germany divided against its will would become unnecessary. At that juncture, a strong and united West would be able to negotiate the economic adjustments and arms agreements attending a reunification settlement.

This was the design, global and long-term. Beyond the most general references to working constructively with the forces of nationalism and liberalization in the Communist bloc, and the assumption that in time East Germany would become a "wasting asset" to Soviet rulers, it contained no hint of initiatives, or the need for them, on reunification. Kennedy's feeling after the Berlin and post-Cuba talks with the Soviets was that while no agreement remotely satisfactory was possible, none was really even necessary, since the situation was finally stable if admittedly imperfect. Remarks from early 1963 tellingly attest to this frame of mind. Apropos of the Multi-lateral Force (MLF), Kennedy said, "The whole debate about an atomic force in Europe is really useless, because Berlin is secure, the Europe as a whole is well protected. What really matters at this point is the rest of the world." Still, he was prepared to let that debate continue, if only to provide the West Germans with an alternative to Gaullism, while conceding that de Gaulle's policy, as exemplified in the Franco-German treaty, was only another means toward the American end of tying "Germany more firmly into the structure of Western Europe."[11] Hence the over-all strategy for East-West relations was accompanied by efforts to keep the Federal Republic a satisfied and contributing member of the Western community in the tasks of maintaining the common defense and establishing a new pattern of relations with the underdeveloped world.

Confronted with this broad and loosely-linked American program for the future, the Federal Republic set about to ensure that its views on the several areas of policy relating to the major concern of reunification were clearly heard. In many ways, this inaugurated the most interesting and fruitful period of adjustment and initiative in Bonn's foreign policy that has been here surveyed, coming as it did in a period of relative relaxation and involving the whole spectrum of issues.

Bonn reiterated the crucial semantic distinction whereby the period was characterized not as one of détente but rather as one of diplomatic soundings to

[11] Schlesinger, *A Thousand Days,* pp. 871–72.

see whether a genuine will to effect a détente actually
existed; as always, the acid test was whether the
shift in Soviet tactics signified a readiness for agreement in Germany or Berlin that did not create new
sources of tension by perpetuating the old and fundamental one of Germany's division. Even in the
absence of direct progress on the German question,
however, Bonn endorsed the Anglo-Americans' efforts on the periphery, such as the nuclear test ban,
and indicated that Germany would consider partial
measures in the area of European security or arms
control which might be advantageous to the alliance.
Adherence to a strict formula was not asked, but
two guidelines were suggested: The measure must
not entail recognition of East Germany, and the
more the current military balance in Europe is altered, the greater would be the requirement for
progress toward political solutions. By these stan-
dards, a nonaggression pact was excluded, except at
the end of a reunification settlement, whereas ground
observation posts were acceptable as a separate
agreement, provided the system was not limited to
German territory alone or tied to a thinning-out or
denuclearization of Central Europe.

A more flexible formula for arms control agreements was complemented by government pronouncements, beginning in 1962, to the effect that mitigat-
ing the human consequences of the German division
was more urgent than overcoming it politically. Generally, this was expressed in formulations in which
Bonn announced it would consider certain sacrifices,
financial among them, if the Soviets would grant the
East German population greater political freedom.
In terms of concrete policy, an ambitious offer by
Adenauer of a ten-year civil peace ending in reuni-

fication went unnoticed by the Soviets, and the principle found its real application subsequently in the more modest efforts to open the Berlin wall for West German visits.

On the broader question of political contacts with Eastern Europe, Foreign Minister Schroeder's much publicized steps to open trade missions with Moscow's allies were a further sign of Bonn's readiness to modify past policies for the period of more active East-West diplomacy that was apparently opening up after the missile crisis and Kennedy's elaboration of a more considered strategy for regulating continuing competition with the Soviet Union. And yet these several indicators of a "policy of movement," so welcome in the West, were never considered in Bonn to be more than a logical complement to continued Western unity and action on reunification. Schroeder himself was emphatic that German policy must probe constantly for openings in the Soviet position, constantly confronting the Kremlin with positive requests for change. Any less active course would entail the danger of allowing people to become accustomed to the division, gradually transforming the status quo into a status quo minus. Thus the Federal Republic could not abandon its calls for a new allied initiative on reunification.

These calls were begun in August, 1963, and repeated many times thereafter, primarily in NATO councils, but they failed to achieve any response above the level of unpublicized departmental deliberations. America's official preference for long-run bridge-building and the absence of allied pronouncements such as the Berlin declaration of 1957 led to some low-key recriminations from Bonn that German unity was being put on ice, that more generally

Washington showed a potentially dangerous tendency to give global concerns priority over European problems lying at the heart of the cold war.

In order to get its prime concern back on the diplomatic agenda, Bonn proposed some variation of the old idea of a permanent four-power commission to consider the German problem. At a minimum, it was hoped that formation of such a body would lead to the establishment of mixed German committees on a parity basis, through which the Federal Republic could work more freely to extend contacts with East Germany beyond economic affairs to travel, cultural and sport exchanges, and a general easing of zonal restrictions. At a maximum, it was hoped that under the auspices of such a forum, designed to evolve procedures leading to reunification, the political, if not final legal, assurances on the borders and armament of a united Germany could be given to the East European countries. The small steps required to prepare for an eventual fusion of the East and West German systems could be expanded and linked to the larger diplomatic issues involved in any over-all settlement. In the absence of such a forum, however, Bonn's rapprochement with the East in the interest of reunification was bound to proceed slowly, if not backfire completely, since every increase in contact with East Germany carried the risk of enhancing the Ulbricht regime, and every concessionary gesture to Germany's eastern neighbors would be misrepresented by the Communists as a step toward recognizing the division.

Unable to engage the allies in serious consideration of new procedures for preparing and defining the contents of a German settlement, Bonn was unwilling to make unilateral and separate revelations of what it would probably concede in exchange for unity, since it was Soviet practice to take such bargaining bids as self-understood preliminary concessions and begin talks with demands for new ones. Statements from West Germany on the great questions of the size, military status, and alignment of a future Germany remained either rigid reminders of the principle, "No concessions without counter-concessions," or vague references to new proposals contained in classified memoranda to the allies. The juncture was unsatisfactory to all but the Communist countries, who kept on unabated with their diatribes against West German militarism and revanchism, while East Germany was unprecedentedly active in shoring up its position as the second sovereign German state with the Soviet Union and the under-developed nations. The campaign to force the West out of Berlin and into relations with Ulbricht had ceased, but the climate of European politics across the demarcation line was still unsettled. Then, in the wake of America's efforts under Kennedy to spearhead a movement toward détente in the period after the Cuban missile crisis, French policy under de Gaulle rapidly crystallized into a series of independent and controversial pronouncements on the unsolved political issues in Europe.

DE GAULLE'S "EUROPEAN" INITIATIVE, 1964–66

The skepticism of the de Gaulle government toward talks with the Russians on anything short of a full German settlement in 1959 became outright opposition to any negotiations at all under pressure during Kennedy's efforts in 1961–62. Commenting on the test ban and optimism about additional great-power agreements, the French President expressed his intention to offer constructive proposals when the day of sincere détente had arrived, but stressed that "for the time being, France will not subscribe to any arrangement that would be made above her head and which would concern Europe and particularly Germany."[12] The French were Germany's staunchest supporters in making Europe practically off-limits to the Anglo-American search for next steps.

In the rapprochement with Bonn coming to fruition at this time, there was a frankly acknowledged element of French self-interest. Consistently de Gaulle had rejected the idea of a neutralized Central Europe in terms of France's simple security from attack, and on the occasion of the Friendship Treaty he extolled Franco-German cooperation as "the most basic factor in the security of our continent and perhaps, in the future, of balance and peace among the nations that people our continent from East to

---

[12] Press Conference of July 29, 1963, *Major Addresses, Statements, and Press Conferences of General Charles De Gaulle,* May 19, 1958–January 31, 1964 (New York: French Embassy, Press and Information Service), p. 235.

West."[13] As much as Dulles, Eden, and Adenauer, de Gaulle felt that West German defection into neutralism would turn the precarious balance decidedly against the West. As much as they, he envisioned the Franco-German reconciliation as an indispensable cornerstone for the greater tasks of building an independent Western Europe and eventually arriving at an all-European settlement, part of which must include German reunification through free elections. But de Gaulle objected to the way traditional Western premises concerning Germany and Europe were being applied in the early 1960's. Uppermost in his mind was the need to explore the possibilities of a lasting East-West accord and, in this regard, he considered German-American policies, in particular, misguided and potentially self-defeating.

Two things, in the French view, prevented the establishment of a more flexible and just equilibrium in Europe: the deadweight of bipolarity, due in part to the American preponderance in the West, and the specter of a German revival. American and West German policy on nuclear sharing, as exemplified by the MLF proposal, had the disastrous consequence of perpetuating both factors simultaneously by prolonging American hegemony and intensifying the fear of Germany. While it is a moot and perhaps decisive question whether de Gaulle was ever willing or able to offer Bonn a substitute for the American nuclear guarantee that the MLF was supposed to cement, it is central to the theme of German reunification in allied diplomacy to note that the French

[13] Press Conference of January 14, 1963, *Major Addresses*, pp. 220–21.

President thought that Atlantic nuclear sharing would complicate indefinitely all attempts to build an independent or even semi-independent center of defense in West Europe, a condition he felt was needed to permit a degree of American withdrawal from continental affairs in the course of settling with the Soviets over Central Europe.

The Americans tended increasingly to value the MLF for the limited purpose of assuring Germany's loyalty to the original alliance. The French, concerned primarily with the effects of NATO policies on East-West relations, stressed the obstacles the arrangement would present for realizing the ultimate aim of ending the continental division. Both governments considered such a settlement a distant prospect at best, but de Gaulle felt more strongly that the need for a more perfect European order should be constantly proclaimed, and that the relationship between short-term expedients and long-term aspirations should never be neglected. These beliefs led during 1964 to the vigorous French campaign aginst the MLF and the surprisingly blunt recital of the inadequacies of Franco-German cooperation as prescribed in the Friendship Treaty. Gaullist diplomacy set about to demonstrate to Bonn and Washington through independent pronouncements and initiatives what it considered to be the proper approach to a real détente on the continent.

Characteristic of the whole enterprise was the lack of any hesitancy to recall publicly that support for West Germany was not unconditional. French interests were defined as three:

> to see that Germany henceforth becomes a definite element of progress and peace; on this condition, to help with its

reunification; to make a start and select the framework which would make this possible.[14]

Kennedy's allusion in 1961 to joint Soviet-American interests in the event of a German revival had held the same ring; the difference lay in the fact that the American President sought to stabilize the situation by coupling arms limitations on the Federal Republic with a Berlin agreement, whereas de Gaulle felt that tinkering with the modalities of the political division would only prolong tension and the concomitant great-power presence. His framework for a German solution was at once more broad than Kennedy's during the Berlin crisis and more precise than that which American policy after Cuba considered possible or worth mentioning. A text for further comments on the French conception of the sequence and substance of a settlement is provided by de Gaulle's most comprehensive statement on the issues involved at his February, 1965, press conference:

> Oh, doubtless, one can imagine things continuing as they are for a long time without provoking ... a general conflagration, since the reciprocal nuclear deterrence is succeeding in preventing the worst. But it is clear that real peace and, even more, fruitful relations between East and West, will not be established so long as the German anomalies, the concern they cause and the suffering they entail continue. It is no less clear that, unless there is fighting .... this matter will not be settled by the direct confrontation of ideologies and forces of the two camps.... What must be done will not be done, one day, except by the un-

[14] De Gaulle Press Conference of February 4, 1965, *Speeches and Press Conferences* (New York: Ambassade de France, Service de Presse et d'Information), #216.

derstanding and combined action of the peoples who have always been, who are and who will remain principally concerned by the fate of the German neighbor—in short, the European peoples. For those peoples to envisage first examining together, then settling in common, and lastly guaranteeing conjointly the solution to a question which is essentially that of their continent—that is the only way that can make reappear, this the only link that can maintain, a Europe in a state of equilibrium, peace and cooperation. . . . the success of such a vast and difficult undertaking implies many conditions. Russia must evolve in such a way that it sees its future . . . through progress accomplished in common by free men and peoples. The nations which it has satellized must be able to play their role in a renewed Europe. It must be recognized, first of all by Germany, that any settlement of which it would be the subject would necessarily imply a settlement of its frontiers and of its armament in agreement with all its neighbors, those on the East and those on the West. The six nations which, let us hope, are in the process of establishing the economic community of Western Europe, must succeed in organizing themselves in the political domain as well as in that of defense, in order to make a new equilibrium possible on our continent.[15]

Central here was the conviction that the division was unbearable because of the suffering it caused and the political progress it prevented, not because the danger of war was acute. Sophisticated arms control measures to defuse the situation, such as the Americans had advocated were considered both unnecessary, given the effectiveness of nuclear deterrence, and, at bottom, irrelevant, given the political roots of tension.

More significant was de Gaulle's emphasis on the European peoples as "primarily concerned." This implied more than simply the irrelevance of Ameri-

[15] *Ibid.*

can ideas; it seemed to denigrate the necessity of the United States taking any direct and primary role in the actual deliberation, negotiation, or enforcement of a settlement. This belief had its most concrete manifestation in French policy toward NATO but entered the reunification debate in the May, 1965, hassle between France and the allies over a declaration endorsing German unity, in which the French wanted a formulation distinguishing European and American interests. The minor episode was symptomatic of de Gaulle's major difficulty: persuading the allies to consider a model of European order other than the modified bipolar system rooted in Western plans and interim policies.

Reference to the regulation of German borders and arms in an East-West forum contained again the narrow European focus thought unwise by the allies, as well as a lamentable lack of precision, in Bonn's view, about the time and place of such concessions. It is almost universally acknowledged that renunciation of the Oder-Neisse territories and strict limitations on German arms will be the condition of any reunification settlement, but only de Gaulle, on this and even more specifically on other occasions, pointedly said so in semi-official announcements, omitting the standard reference to one grand peace conference. Whatever the immediate repercussions of such gestures to the East on Franco-German cooperation in building the more independent Western Europe that French policy clearly understands as the basis for wider continental accords, de Gaulle held considered candor essential in the meantime lest the progressive consolidation in the West prolong suspicions and hold the East-West rapprochement in abeyance. These unorthodox gestures increased during 1965, to be climaxed by the even more dramatic actions of the following year—France's withdrawal from NATO integration, and de Gaulle's visit to Moscow.

These French policies seemed to the majority of policy-makers in Britain, Germany, and America to place the whole structure of postwar Western diplomacy in jeopardy. The secession from NATO seemed designed to diminish the alliance's effectiveness to such a degree that the Soviets would be induced to make a separate deal with the French over the future status of the continent. France's allies forgot that the British had gone unilaterally to Moscow in 1959, and in 1961 had counseled negotiations in a time of utmost tension while denying the need to raise the military ante. They forgot that the Americans, too, had sought high level talks without an increase in military outlays in 1959 and later under Kennedy had pushed on with bilateral negotiations in spite of French and German reluctance. De Gaulle's maverick course in 1966 was seen as a unique threat to the traditional means of allied policy—a strong NATO—and as a unique departure from its traditional procedure—unity in dealing with the enemy.

And yet the Moscow venture showed, even if in radically altered circumstances from the Geneva meetings of a decade before, that the essentially political fact of the German division still remained the core problem of the East-West conflict, the acknowledged and unchanged issue by which to test the possibility of far-reaching changes. What had Dulles done eleven years earlier but play his record on Germany while the Soviets played theirs?

De Gaulle was willing to travel alone, to ostracize

himself from Western officialdom on the questions of the alliance's strength and structure and the size and strength of a future Germany, but he was not willing to abandon the goal of reunification on the basis of self-determination. Indeed, he was far less ready than American and British governments in the past to consider makeshift arrangements that endangered the goal by lending legitimacy to the East German regime, although his statements could easily be construed to imply a most evolutionary view of how the division would be overcome. No more than Adenauer, Macmillan, or Kennedy before him was he able to solve the issue alone. But in 1966 he had become the Western statesman for whom an agreement on Germany was a pressing necessity, and he had a deeper grasp of the essentials of the problem and the limits of political compromise in arranging a settlement than any allied leaders except the Germans. Leaving aside the question of ultimate motives, the complicated and ambiguous relationship between the French and European aspects of de Gaulle's design, we can say for our purposes that he was as diplomatically interested in progress toward reunification as any Western statesman before him. His endeavors testified to the enduring if not exclusive presence of German reunification in Western diplomacy.

V. REMARKS ON THE PRESENT JUNCTURE

The American reaction to French policy reflected a continued concern with Germany, too, albeit in a much more familiar manner. Loyally, the United States refrained from blunt talk about the concessions a settlement would require and soft-pedaled without formally abandoning the search for allied nuclear sharing. But for all practical purposes its policy on reunification had become geared almost solely to the little steps and long time necessary for a strategy of "environmental improvement" in East-West relations. The real though muted concern of American and British policy-makers was that de Gaulle's unilateralist example was premature and would set the West Germans off on their own to the East. While acknowledging the need for a more active Eastern policy, someday, the Anglo-American powers fell back on the incontestable principle that a strong and united West was the precondition for a successful policy of détente. In fact, their interest in maintaining traditional NATO solidarity stemmed from an overriding desire to keep West Germany stable and predictable. At a minimum it was assumed that the Federal Republic had become adjusted to the split and that the alliance continued to serve her more fundamental interests by providing military security. At a maximum, the unsolved issues surrounding Germany were recalled, and the necessity of keeping them in view as part of the longer range movement toward détente was underlined. The status quo was declared unsatisfactory, as always, but there was no compulsion to insist on a broad rethinking of Western strategy as de Gaulle had done, no impetus to reopen debate with the Soviet Union on the basis of older arguments. The hard-won stability that followed the Berlin and Cuban confrontations became the measure of the acceptable as well as the possible in the European stalemate.

De Gaulle, too, valued the alliance in part as a constraint on Germany, but, significantly, his government placed particular insistence on the preservation of the juridical principle of four-power responsibility for a final settlement embodied in the Paris agreements of 1954. This made West Germany's position toward French diplomacy fundamentally ambivalent. De Gaulle's willingness to keep the reunification issue alive in talks with the Communist bloc was welcome, while the wider implications of his NATO and European policies for the security of the Federal Republic and the adequacy of a final solution were a source of great controversy and apprehension.

The Erhard government attempted to compensate for the disappearance of a common Western diplomacy on reunification with renewed reminders and suggestions of its own. On the time and place of a settlement, Bonn continued to argue against the consignment of reunification to the glacial movements of history, conceding that while unity would not come about as the result of a single summit, it nonetheless would have to emerge from a series of multilateral conferences at which the interrelated political, economic, and military issues were treated together. In its last major initiative, the peace note of the spring of 1966, Erhard's administration endeavored to maintain a focus of constructive attention on the unsolved problems in Central Europe by endorsing compromise formulas for nonaggression pacts, progress toward a nuclear free zone, and exchanges of military observers with Warsaw Treaty powers. All of these were Eastern bloc ideas which until then had been considered unacceptable in their proposed form, but had never been answered with counterproposals.

As always, Bonn hesitated to spell out major concessions in the military realm before political agreements were reached, on the grounds that these would be construed by friends and enemies alike as currently applicable restrictions. The basic political constraints on such initiatives also remained: the continued refusal to recognize East Germany and to abandon the legal principle that Germany's current borders were only provisional, pending regulation at a final peace conference. But within the limits thus maintained, there was greater flexibility and concreteness in spelling out acceptable measures for disarmament and security arrangements, even prior to political agreements. This tendency was especially marked because the practice of endorsing the current Western package had become less satisfactory; first with the relative decline of American interest in Europe, thereafter with the growing divergence of French policy from previously accepted Western designs and procedures. Increasingly, West Germany had to speak and act for itself in foreign affairs, and the failure of Chancellor Erhard to rise quickly and competently enough to the necessity contributed heavily to the fall of his government in late 1966.

The Kiesinger-Brandt coalition which emerged is as much a sign of the continuing deadlock in German foreign and domestic policy as it is the result of a

clear reaction to the situation of confused *immobil-
isme* over which Erhard presided. The inconsistencies and contradictions that plague the Federal Republic's actions in the three main areas of West
European, East European, and Atlantic policy will
not be cleanly resolved on the basis of an unequivo-
cal national mandate for change. Opinion remains
unsettled, and Germany's unalterable position as the
"land in the middle" admits of no simple solutions.
There exists rather only a common desire among
politicians and populace for a more vigorous and
differentiated German policy in all directions—toward America, toward France, toward the great
complex of problems confronting any attempts to influence Moscow and East Europe—in pursuit of the
still proclaimed goal of achieving national unity. The
mending of Franco-German relations and the candid
airing of problems with the United States show
definite shifts of emphasis, as do the attempts to
establish diplomatic relations with Moscow's allies.

This radical revision of the Hallstein doctrine is
a departure from past policy of major political sig-
nificance. While clearly an admission that the self-
denying ordinance has come to cost German policy
in East Europe far more than it returns, it an-
nounces at the same time Bonn's active entry into the
renascent diplomatic arena. Increasingly, since
Schroeder became foreign minister, the Federal Republic had shown an intensified awareness of the
need for a more dynamic and conciliatory Eastern
policy in order to prepare the ground for possible
reunification much in the way that Bonn's rehabili-
tation within the Western political community had
been achieved. Under the Kiesinger-Brandt coalition, this broad rationale remains, while the politi-

cal environment has become even more conducive to ventures in the East with the elaboration of American and particularly French formulas for the revitalization of bilateral ties with the Communist bloc. Hopefully for Germany, it is easier now than in the past to justify such actions at home and to legitimize them abroad.

The search for increased influence and respectability in East Europe remains for the moment subordinated to past theses of reunification policy. It is unlikely that Bonn will be prepared to grant immediately and directly the three conditions that the Eastern bloc countries would set ideally as the price for the resumption of diplomatic relations—a West German recognition of East Germany, acceptance of the Oder-Neisse line, and renunciation of nuclear weapons. In the establishment of ties with Rumania, all of these issues were avoided; subsequent negotiations will of course become progressively difficult as Budapest, Prague, and then Warsaw are approached. With each prospective partner, the issues will have to be dealt with in a different fashion.

One requirement of the new Eastern policy clearly understood in Bonn is the need for more conclusive declarations on the legal invalidity of the Munich agreement and more convincing political disavowals of any claim to repossession of the Oder-Neisse territories. Officials in Bonn are also considering various new interim relationships with East Germany, as well as unorthodox models of a finally acceptable settlement. Here, however, less probability of an early consensus exists. The Kiesinger-Brandt government is more committed than either of its predecessors to actually defining and pursuing a policy based on the principle, first enunciated by Adenauer in 1958, that concern for the freedom of the seventeen million East Germans must take precedence over efforts to regain the nation's juridical unity. This statement of the problem permits speculation of real political relevance on a possible "Austrian" solution to the entire German question, or even a "Yugoslavian" status for East Germany, to name only two alternatives.

Germany under the new government is undertaking on its own to reconsider and reshape its policies and relationships in all facets of foreign policy. While the outcome of a more independent, flexible, and imaginative West German diplomacy cannot be foreseen, major changes will certainly occur in the approach to reunification, where Bonn's actions have for so long been predicated on the existence of commonly accepted theses and priorities, jointly pursued or at least defended, by the Western allies. The minimal aim of the new government is to achieve more scope for political maneuver in the quest for unity without abandoning the several legal positions concerning the necessity and nature of a final settlement. To date, the policy changes represent only a procedural departure from the course adopted in the early years of the Federal Republic's membership in NATO. In time, however, they may become more than primarily tactical and defensive adjustments, to the degree that the high promise of the original Western design for overcoming the cold war in Europe becomes less convincing. No longer is there a Western orthodoxy. Major initiatives by Kennedy and de Gaulle to restructure the Atlantic relationship for altered circumstances have been but symptoms of the need for new directions, not well-laid paths or even commonly acknowledged signposts.

No NATO country can now avoid what has been a chronic controversy for Bonn; namely, whether the pursuit of security and encouragement of economic and political unity in Western Europe are incompatible with a reconciliation embracing the entire continent. West Germany's acute and specific dilemmas —America or France, security or reunification, ideological cohesion or national unity—have always expressed in miniature the latent inconsistencies embedded in Western actions since the war.

Too frequently the choices facing the West are stated in so broad and bland a manner that the answers seem self-evident: It is proposed that the alliance transfer its concern from the military realm to the political, in order to become an agent for détente rather than deterrence; that the Germans concede that NATO does not guarantee reunification, and begin to plan in terms of long-term changes in inter-bloc relations rather than maintain the fiction of a final grand peace conference. When one abandons prescription by platitude and attempts to formulate more sharply what the execution of such advice might entail, the alternatives assume the character of hard dilemmas. An alliance for détente might require a demonstrative decrease of American power and influence in European affairs, following, if not preceding, a significant increase in military cooperation on the continent itself. This has heretofore been considered acceptable only if a united Europe were in existence, or, given its absence, if Franco-British cooperation formed the nuclear cornerstone. Such are the actual security concerns, however, that Germany, and not Britain, is most in need of France as a partner in future defense arrangements, and the French have notoriously little confidence in Britain's readiness to help replace the American guarantee. The deadlock is as much a political as a technical one.

Similarly, for Germany to become more realistic about the necessity for a gradual approach to East-West relations is usually taken to mean that Bonn should assume diplomatic relations with Eastern Europe, while progressively expanding technical contacts with East Germany until a degree of liberalization resulted that would make political recognition palatable. Yet a concomitant of this process might be a period of intense political competition as the two systems sought, in the manner of political parties, to win the populace over on the issues under debate. It must be underlined that even if the questions of the Oder-Neisse line and access to nuclear weapons were clarified beforehand by West Germany in the way desired by the majority of governments and commentators in East and West alike, the German problem would not simply disappear in a mass of cultural exchanges, diplomatic discourse, and trade. The Soviet Union, the Eastern European states, and the two German regimes are well aware that the ultimate source of conflict is over the constitution of the German body politic itself. The ceaseless tirades from the East against Bonn's border claims and nuclear aspirations serve also as first lines of defense for the Ulbricht regime. The bloc countries could not conceivably be indifferent to the example and outcome of renewed competition between the Eastern and Western systems on German soil, no matter how carefully circumscribed that competition might be in terms of the territorial extent and weaponry of the possibly emergent political unit. The Russian and East German decision to cancel the

speaker exchange demonstrated this, while the episode showed conversely the zest for a real political
contest present in the Federal Republic. The expan-
sion of East-West contacts that seems so desirable
and stabilizing in the abstract would spell not the
end but the onset of an era of competitive political
coexistence in Europe.

The problems associated with Germany's continuing partition reflect in essence those of the par-
titioned European continent. As West German policy questions the relevance of the reunification
settlement proposed in 1955, and the adequacy of
the 1954 Paris agreements as the framework for
efforts aimed at reunification, it mirrors the transitional state of all Western thought and action concerning the future of East-West relations.